THE VERY RICH HOURS

THE VERY RICH HOURS

GREGORY LOSELLE

A Publication of The Poetry Box®

©2019 Gregory Loselle
All rights reserved.

Editing & Book Design by Shawn Aveningo Sanders
Cover Design by Robert R. Sanders
Author Photo (original painting) by Ian Burk

No part of this book may be reproduced in any manner whatsoever without permission from the author, except in the case of brief quotations embodied in critical essays, reviews and articles.

ISBN: 978-1-948461-43-6
Library of Congress Control Number: 2019907780

Printed in the United States of America.

Published by The Poetry Box©, 2019
Beaverton, Oregon
ThePoetryBox.com

"... And even if you found yourself in some prison, whose walls let in none of the world's sound—wouldn't you still have your childhood, that jewel beyond all price, that treasure house of memories?"

—Rilke, *Letters to a Young Poet*

Contents

The Very Rich Hours

Learning to Shave	11
The Snake in the Holly	12
Triolets at Mid-Morning	13
Oracle	14
The Magnolia and the Telephone: Spring View from the Den Window	15
Rondeaux de Chambre: Barbara's Room	16
Crossing to Fox Island	19
Attic Heat: A Jumbled Inventory	21
The Fortune-Tellers	24
The Mystery of the Linen Closet	25
A Paint-Crate of Photographs	27
Shelling in the Philippines, World War II	29
Dark Matter: The Den Closet	31
Microscopy	32
The Furnace Room	33
Porch Light Carnival	34
Walking the Dog on the Milky Way	35
The Boat-Hoist *De Profundis*	36
Our Musical Heritage: Time-Life's Great Recordings of the Classics	38
The Living Room at Night	39
Dreaming the Animal Parade	40

After-Hours

A String, a Frame, a Tail	43
Semi-Private Room	46
Lost and Found	49
The Second Wife	53
The Sister-in-Law Sells Off the China: a Ballade	54
The Theft of the Pears	55
Walking through the Empty House	57

✷ ✷ ✷

Acknowledgments	61
Praise for *The Very Rich Hours*	65
About the Author	67
About The Poetry Box®	69

The Very Rich Hours

Learning to Shave

Drawing water into lather
with his brush, the alchemist
spins the handle with his wrist.
I watch the foaming bubbles gather

within the filling porcelain mug.
I'd inherit that same gesture—
stirring from my wrist the water
into foam—the round cake sunk

beneath the suds. I'd watch him shaving
Sunday mornings as a child,
sitting on the sink, beguiled
by ritual, anticipating

first the foaming mug and lathered
face, the razor, then the scraping
off of stubble. Later, aping
him, I learned to shave—I gather

this is how all boys behave
at first—bowing to the mirror
as I remembered my grandfather
did—as did his own—half awed

and half embarrassed. This is how
we go about it, mimicry
across the generations—see
my hands? I watch and see his, now.

The Snake in the Holly

It doesn't matter that the neighbors came
and after shouts and blows the snake
was lifted, broken, on the blade of a hoe;
or where the snake was flung,
under which shrub, or what's become
of its dry skin, its fine bones and eyes.

What mattered is what the boy saw
as his grandmother hurried him out
the door, and cried out, and pointed
and shrank away but couldn't look away,
held by the twisting thing advancing.
What matters is that he still glances
down the snake's lost track today.

Triolets at Mid-Morning

I

The children gone, the house resumes
a contemplation of itself,
a meditative index, croons
The children gone! Then it resumes
enumerating baby spoons
and cataloging toys on shelves.
The children? Gone! The house resumes
a contemplation of itself.

II

The tapping of the heating pipes
within their radiating ruffs—
the beating wind on windows snipes
its tapping echo. Heating pipes
and whistles through the house and gripes
behind the paneling: the soughs
of tapping in the heating pipes
within the radiators, rough.

III

Bright sunlight on a windowsill
creeps west to east, glows in the leaves
of houseplants, yellows papers still
spread open on the table. *Will
blank crossword puzzle spaces fill
themselves?* the sharpened pencil grieves.
Bright sunlight on the windowsill
creeps westward, glowing as it leaves.

ORACLE

The fireplace exhales the memory of heat,
the odor of ash and trapped air.

The books, a silent chorus on the shelves
shrug off their titles; closed, they stare

and speak no judgment. A stack of magazines
ages on the floor, compact in its despair.

A pen on the desk points through the window,
toward the yard. Who left it there?

The Magnolia and the Telephone
Spring View from the Den Window

The magnolia tree holds promise of the promises of spring:
blooms thick in the warming air, earth's scent transfiguring
into flesh, the resurrection exacting buried seeds from buds.

Electric lines pierce the dark crown, draw current down
through knotted arms they chafe against, transporting pulse
from root to blossom, above the drive and into the house.

Conversation over wire is not immune to whispers inching
up the trunk, conducting out through leaves, into air:
both arch above leaf-patterns on the drive, the stir

of sound outside. The tree's shed fleshy petals rot and smear
the blacktop, dry and blow away. The line is clear.

Rondeaux de Chambre: Barbara's Room

I

In Barbara's room the bride doll leans
askew, its legs thrust out. It seems
to raise one arm, if less to bless
or gesture in wide-eyed protest,
than stay the afternoon's esteem

discovered in snagged lace and cream
sateen in sunlight—what she means,
both in her presence and her dress,
in Barbara's room,

uncertain. Witnessing the scene
with her, imagine Barbara Jean
long gone—the bottles on the dresser
drained, stuffed animal confessors
fallen mute, the bride serene
in Barbara's room.

II

In Barbara's room her old guitar
waits out the afternoon, aware
of stilled vibrations in its strings
where lost, potential music rings
in silence in the silent air,

and melodies unheard repair
to memory. Old songs despair—
for now, at least, nobody sings
in Barbara's room.

Consider this: the old guitar
is waiting for another player;
the instrument untouched bides time,
untuning in the corner. I'm
too young, yet, for the old guitar
in Barbara's room.

III

In Barbara's room, the canopy
above the bed hangs limpidly,
unstirring in the unstirred air.
The *papier maché* tortoise stares
from underneath the vanity.

Her perfume bottles all agree
among themselves: their tragedy
lies in being abandoned there
in Barbara's room.

Her books, her dolls, her diary,
her correspondence, jewelry—
or what at least she didn't care
to pack and take away with her—
is left behind for all to see
in Barbara's room.

Crossing to Fox Island

Every act is first an act of faith:
One foot, slowly, lowered to the ice,
And then the other foot, and then we stand
Above the vault the river winters under;

And look across the flat unreal expanse,
Imagination telling us we cannot stand
Where water ought to be—where water is
Beneath us. Then we start across the ice.

Some patches, dark and flat, are panes of glass,
Like windows into night beneath our feet,
Where trapped air scatters from our steps
Reminding us that we are more like stones

Than shadows, howsoever lightly
We might cross above the shuttered flow
And tread the temporary span from land
To island. Snow abrades the most of it:

Bright crusty scabs that crumble underfoot,
And leave us gasping, stumbling in the space
Below the space we occupied, reminded
Of the weight above the depths below.

One inch will hold one walker, if he's light,
And two a group, and three or four a car:
We counted out the thickness as we dressed
And count it as we walk across it now,

[. . .]

And onto land again, the island's crested beach,
The trees that rise among the drifts. And looking back
We measure out the distance, trace our tracks,
Where every act of faith was first an act.

Attic Heat: A Jumbled Inventory

I

Bundled in the jumbled luggage,
the squares of an unassembled afghan,
pink and crimson, bed the brittle needles,
soft as chalk, yellowed as old ivory aging
in heat, awaiting disposition. What's knitted's
knotted in the memory, forgot but not untied.

The untied squares await memory,
unassembling in the jumbled luggage.
Pink, soft as chalk, and needling crimson
knit the afghan's brittle bed, old forgotten ivory
bundled in the knotted yellow heat.

The needles, brittle as chalk,
knit age into ivory-yellow heat, await
the untied crimson dispositions, forget
the knotted afghan, their jumbled bed,
the soft pink bundles of unassembled memory.

Forget memory, brittle and soft as ivory:
the knitted afghan bundles and crimson
needles bed old knots untied, not disposed
but aging pink and waiting in the jumble
of unassembled squares, the luggage
yellow in the chalky heat.

[. . .]

II

The metal shelf spills unruly volumes
in stacks across the plank floor,
heavy textbooks and open novels
underlined and noted, the sweet
scent of browned pulp rising
in the dark air, moted and dry.

Dry volumes in the unruly air:
dark stacks of texts, open, underline
the browning planks, the floor,
books on the shelves note
the metal scent, spilled across planks,
raising pulp-sweet motes.

The unruly floor rises, spilling open
stacks of noted textbooks, underlining
the dark metal shelves, the pulp-brown
novels and dry planks heavy
with dark motes, the volumes
dry-scented and sweet.

The heavy scent spills across the air:
a dry and unruly volume in the dark;
motes underlie the planks, the stacks,
the novels, the metal shelf open
and noted: texts rising across
the book-sweet brown floor.

III

Past the reach of the wooden boards
where insulation foams between the joists,
Peggy's presents outlast the wedding,
nestled in tissue paper, shining in the shadows
a flashlight throws into the tapering space.

The past foams in the tapering space,
outlasting the wooden boards. Shining
presents nest in insulation, flash light
onto the joists, reach through the wooden
shadows of Peggy's tissue-paper wedding.

Shadows light the foam, past the spaces
tapering to the present. Peggy's flashlight
shines on insulation and tissue paper
reaching out from the wedding, at last,
nested between the joists, bored.

Shadow is the tissue of the past. The tapering
light flashes, reaches the shining presents,
nestles in the foam of last weddings. Peggy,
in the joists and paper insulation,
bears out the presents.

The Fortune-Tellers

On the white formica, the fan of cards
she cheats with, spreading three faces
up instead of one, piles into a heap
beside the ashtray. The radio recounts
a conversation overheard and unimportant. Rain
is promised, threatened, ignored. He's reading

As You Like It on the couch—or less reading
than resenting Jacques' lines. The cards
buckle and snap, bowed in her hands. Their faces
absorbed in pattern, repetition, plot. Heap
all of these Saturday afternoons together, recount
them one by one: they all rain

down much the same. It is always about to rain.
He is always reading. She is always playing cards
alone, or more alone for the faces
he pulls: teenage boredom, thick-heaped
in the room, estranging her. Reading
past his concentration, she recounts

the time the girls dressed the dog in jewelry, recounts
how it ran away and stayed until rain
drove it home in rhinestones and water-spangles. The cards
align in columns: solitaire, a memory. They face
the same conundrum different ways: the clock reading
off the unfilled hours, time piling in heaps

before and behind them. She has a game, he a heap
of aspirations: grand, callow, reading
a script he won't completely master, re-counting
the minutes pared from the hour, raining
into the lines his fool's prospective glory. The cards
accumulate, numbers in a ledger, the tallies facing

credits or debits to their accounts. *Face
it for once*, I could shout to myself, *you can heap
up your defenses, ignore the weather, reading
now into forever. You can spend your life recounting
afternoons you read and sulked and she smoked and rain
blew in.* She shuffles the cards.

He sighs and gives up reading. "Here comes the rain,"
she says, recounting the deck by threes, face
up, stacked in a heap, our lives in the cards.

The Mystery of the Linen Closet

One twenty-dollar bill laid flat
in the folds of a linen tablecloth
outlasts the hand that hid it.

A gray leaf raked loose in spring,
fluttering on the air, catching a corner
on the floor, falling, unexpected:
the currency of our straightening,
a riddle for our recounting.

Most hidden things are meaningless—
no matter that we strive to think
the gift uncovered comes wrapped up
in suppositions thin as ironed cloth,
folded into panes and laid away, waiting
for us when we open the door
and speak the approved text.

But some deepen further in revelation:
the answer, casting off its cerements,
falls between us on the carpet, asks
to hear what we already know.

A Paint-Crate of Photographs

I

Pictures in the hallway closet
call us to forgotten places,
store the backyard summer sunlight,
eternize the children's faces,

quarantine the Christmas parties,
memorialize vacations,
revive the dead and cast-off houseplants,
ratify our reservations,

press in yellowing celluloid amber
we've forgotten what or who,
age us gently and remind us
what we were and meant to do.

II

Negatives inside a packet
of waxed paper cancel light,
changing what we don't remember
from full daylight into night.

Darkness haunts the celebrations,
blackface ghosts bewail the sight:
trees in blossom weather winter
uncomplaining of their plight.

Undeveloped, slick, transparent,
reds are greens, the moon's the sun;
negatives unnerve and tell us
what we never could have done.

Shelling in the Philippines, World War II

The spoils of war—or at least some of them—
are wrapped in khaki socks and paper sacks
gone greasy-soft, and one tobacco tin
(*of course he never smoked—how'd that get in?*),
some other soldier cast-off on a beach
from which he snorkeled. That was war to him:
short on heroics, long on medicine,

long in the afternoons and short on ills
exotic, catastrophic or extreme.
He'd set out once the morning's needs were filled:
elastic bandages and quinine pills
gave way to sunlit shallows and the gleam
of plundered shells—anemone's dark quills
as thin as fine cigars, the queen conch frilled

along her lip and crowned above, cats' eyes
(some buffed with jeweler's rouge, some dull
with frosted pupils)—booty of his dives
in Filipino waters. Other lives
were tenanted inside those turban shells
that rattled in our fingers. Creatures live
and hidden curving shelves contrived

for underwater habitation. Now,
not forty years gone since, he takes them out,
unfolds the rags they swaddle in, and how
he harvested this sunken treasure, how
he shipped them back secreted in his kit
and, disembarked at last in New Orleans,
he stowed them on the transport train, recounts—

[. . .]

as I count shells and beg for one or two—
the epic of his wartime past. Each day
a letter home to Fay included clues
to where he was. Each day's tattoo
of offshore guns discharging practice rounds
above the blue Pacific—these things, too,
survive inside the shells' pearlescent blue

interiors like whispers down a hall
around a turn. The abalone's gray
and vibrant moiré satin lining palls
the memory. Shells echo lives, recall
the two-day's train ride northward by northeast,
recall the stations and the cab, recall
the beach they left behind them, after all.

All epics are about our coming home.
All treasures are composed of what survives
to be retold again, all journeys, lone
or in the company of others—known
itineraries, oceans decades wide
between, eventually all we own—
become at last the shell we call our home.

Dark Matter: The Den Closet

"The camera huddles in its leather case, its face an eye,
its eye a lens, its heart a darkened chamber."
—Brendan Cahalan

The camera in its leather case turns inward
past its lapsed shutter, dreaming of lightless
cave-born fishes luminescent in sightless
deep water dark, wary creatures, filmed
eyes hid like the oculi of moles or grubs
or worms who know only thick earth dark,
or nuzzled snugly underneath the bark.

Propped on metal legs, the telescope cranes
toward the closet's upmost reach, strains its sights
past the speech of gears and mirrors. Its need
recalls the heavy moon's full round, the lost face
magnified, its ranges sharp-defined, scarred
sea-reaches dry and clearer to the mind
than to the uninstructed eye. It knows the need
to see what is obscured: it knows the fever,
and it craves the fever cured.

In bottles on the closet floor, boxed or lolling
on the rug, softening corks ruddy whites;
particulates like cells in serum distill in sedimental
reds, drifting into muddy heaps and dunes
that drift along the curving darkened glass insides,
while aging out the changes life contrives.

Microscopy

The moon is populous tonight: the spotlight
clots with drifting globes, the fruit of hidden vines,
pressed between the slide and frost-thin pane
flattening drops of blood.

The moon is populous tonight. The turned brass
dial, its edges milled, sharpens the circle, lifts
jumbled colors into definition: dark sap
pricked from his grandfather's fingertip
extrudes an evening's entertainment.

Cells collide and drift and dodge the squinting
lashes' tangles, pile up, dying on the slide. Inside
their coded centers threads of color recombine
the blood the boy observes, derives, cultivates

beneath his own skin, membranes thin
and supple, capillaries branching out
beyond the circle's the rim. The moon
is populous tonight, both outside and within.

The Furnace Room

The furnace room is hot. Its air, compressed,
occludes the ticking of the pipes, the valves'
impassive beat. The pilot lights invest
themselves—first glow and flicker, duck and calf
blue flashes in the dark—and then are spent
in summoning the warm rust-scent that choirs
and pulses through the gloom; *This time is lent,*
expounds the water-heater, *What transpires
here next is warming in the viscera.*
A gauge displays within its grimed glass eye
its capillary rage, the temperature
of water pressure-pent. The boiler sighs
and coughs. *We serve,* it says, *we do not care;
what sympathy within the heart laid bare?*

Porch Light Carnival

Pulled into orbit, each speck, flying
half-brightened in the threat of night,
describes an arc around the light, in thrall
and vassalage, caught moons and meteorites.

Seen through the screen, the yellow bulb collects
furred nets of old webs, spun halos of buzzing
dust-brown moths and the gritty shells of gnats
and mosquitoes in the hot click of impact.

Indolent spiders with no desire to crack
the glass carapace and dive, antennae
first, into the light of immolation, crouch
and spin and trap and glut themselves.

Each night the light returns to webs rattle-strung
with hollow shells and shed wings, insect souls
cast off where insect hope and insect death
meet and feast arachnid avarice.

Walking the Dog on the Milky Way

The street is really little more than road
paved over, hunched and starting to erode

in patches where the macadam is dark
like water pooled. In starting to erode,

soft chunks break free and crumble into grit.
I walk around them. Starting to erode,

the way ahead, by flashlight or by moon,
lies maculate and, starting from the road,

the dog takes off, its barking startling us,
out after a rabbit startled too. A road

careers above us through the sky, its way
as patchy as our own. Stars light two roads—

there's one before us, one above as well:
Canus, gemini—stars: and two a-road.

The Boat-Hoist *De Profundis*

The cables stir the water underneath
the dock, beneath our feet. Waves thud and slap
and then erupt between the planks in sprays
of drops and darkening foam dissolving back
into the deep we stand above.
                                        He lifts
me up to press the button—red and wide
enough for two thumbs, his and mine (because
I'm seven, maybe, and not strong enough)
to hold it down and keep it down—which starts
the motor, sets the winch to turn, and pulls
the platform of the hoist above the waves.

The boat first frets its cradle, ducks and nods
its bow at us—penned living in the well,
moored in repining restlessness and urged
to shoulder up against the wooden stiles
by troubling heaves—then settles, grounds itself
secure, surrendering, now a member of
the mechanism of the hoist.
                                    The torque
of cables tunes them to the winch. They cough
and bark and chime; they wind themselves around
the drum in tightening spirals as they pluck
a rusting melody out of their depths
and stresses. Strains and accidentals clang
and echo as the metal fibers toll
out every inch above the lowering stir;
their pitches bend, contracting to a span
the burden of the boathouse and the well.

The boat secure, he switches off the light
and carries me back up the hill. The house
shines out impassively above: all's well
again, it says, above the glass-dark swell.

Our Musical Heritage
Time-Life's Great Recordings of the Classics

The boy abed, Joe puts the record on
And leaves the room and, turning off the light,
he lets it play. The child becomes the song

he hears, the music as he settles down
into dream-shallows from the wakeful heights.
The boy in bed, Joe puts the record on

and, leaving, shuts the door. The sound
expands and, reaching through contracting night,
hearing it play, the child becomes the song

the way its music fills the air: the sound
a pattern in the dark, its pulse alight
the boy in bed. Joe puts the record on

and wanders off to other things. The long
entangling lines of violin delight
the boy. He lets it play, becomes the song

he'll carry through his life—this song the one
he still comes home to, still, awake at night
lying in bed. Joe put the record on
and let it play. The boy became the song.

The Living Room at Night

In the living room, the couch and chairs
sit out the night in conversation, the coffee
table caught between. Words filter into walls
and cushions, pen the memory of springs
compressed, re-enact our thoughts in tufted
patterns and upholstered folds. The fireplace
gapes, sentinel, its ashes evening evidence.

Moonlit windows enlarge against the furniture,
press against Marilyn's portrait over the piano,
marshal the pattern of the carpet into pale trapezoids
askew the door. Other rooms breathe and rustle, turn
dumbly in their sleep and fall quiet once more.

From the kitchen the refrigerator tunes its pitch,
the digital clock clicks off minutes with a soft
resolve; numbers, wheels and gears revolve,
and water pumped through walls to radiant
baseboards gushes and pours. Pilot lights ignore
other rooms' cries and snores.

But in the living room, a book lies flatly
on the floor, matter-of-factly saying, *I know
the corridor, I know its narrow floor, and
I know which cries to answer, which to ignore.*

Dreaming the Animal Parade

They took the wakeful child into their bed
and laid him—restless, small—between them there,
and wandered back to sleep. But he, awake,
imagines animals in slow parade

from far across the lawn, from out of night,
advancing toward the window, sauntering
toward him—the wolf, the lion, polar bear:
imagined animals in slow parade,

each one evaporating in the dark
and dreamful scene outside. No creature climbs
the sill or rises up and looks inside—
all wander off to sleep. The boy, awake,

knows he is dreaming, still the dark is charmed
by willful fantasy: he can't fulfill
the duties of unconsciousness. He calls to those
who laid him—restless, small—between them there,

who stir and close the drapes, close out the night
and, coming back to bed, resume their sleep.
Years later, they'll recall how, with delight,
they took the wakeful child into their bed.

After-Hours

A String, A Frame, A Tail

A String

Consider how a kite struck from the sky
collapses on itself and creases up
in flight: a battered bird, a broken hand,
a sail unfurled and rippling as it falls;

and notice how it settles—not quite falls—
onto the ground. Our kite descended to
a stubble-field and folded in a heap,
white struts askew and blaze-orange mylar wings

like crumpled sparrow-bones, like monarchs' wings
torn off: a crumpled origami crane,
a surplus constellation cast away,
consigned untraced to earth. The accident,

the intervention of coincident
effects (a plane come burgeoning through haze,
the rumble of its engines rumpling up
the evening air before the fuselage

sailed into view, its wings and fuselage
pale silver in the silver sky, props blurred,
the spray it dusted fluming up behind,
the kite colliding with its wing) first shocked

[. . .]

and then confounded us. We stood, both, shocked
and, watching, felt the acrid chemical
descending through the air. And then, our skin

embittered with insecticide, we crossed
the lot along the string that led across
the space we'd sought to fly a kite from, rode
the long electrocardiographic line
to terminus beneath the poisoned sky.

A Frame

That night in Georgetown, stumbling, dinner-drunk,
out of the restaurant, into the street
and down the block in muggy summer heat,

we paused before the window of a shop
lit springtime-bright by incandescent light
through nylon kites as bright as kites

at night can be in summer's mild twilight,
and pondered for a moment, then went in
and stood among the struts and staves and trim,

and gaped at color for its own sake, gaped
at shapes designed to craftily beguile
the breeze to cheat earth's gravity as well

as lift the eye aloft. A widower
just four months upwind of your obsequies,
and I, aggrieved as only youth could be,

and leaving soon for college in this strange
new city—how we tore ourselves away
and wandered out, or what we had to say,

I don't recall—but do remember this:
in a kite-shop in the darkening summer night
we found sufficient—we, then, there—delight.

A Tail

A kite's an upward embassy,
an emissary to the sky
from earth, from where we stand below
and stare up, grounded as we fly.

A kite's a tugging of the string
that leads us upward, toward the sky.
a kite's an answer to the thing
we asked, and then decided to let lie.

A kite's a stay against the wind.
A kite's a snag pulled from the sky.
A kite's a little, leaving thing
that rises, then diminishes, then dies.

Semi-Private Room

I

My mother's in the hallway on the phone,
so loud I wince. Inside your room, alone
with you, I look away from your veiled stare,
your open mouth, the morphine drip, the snare
back of your throat that catches at each breath,
the half-drawn blinds, the prospect of your death.

You'd asked me if the nurses were awake.
You'd fretted at the catheter. You'd speak
in acronyms and riddles, didn't know
the day or date—and knew you didn't know.
But when they wheeled the morphine in and sent
the fluid through your veins, you welcomed it.

Now when they speak to you, they shout. They use
your first name. I, indignant, tell the nurse,
*It's Doctor, not just Joe. Cahalan. Don't you know
this building's named for him? A month from now's
the dedication.* But he only shrugs and stares.
I've never heard the name, he says, and leaves.

I sit and fume. My mother, on the phone
outside, is rattling off the news. The drone
of the machine that monitors your heart
engulfs the room, bright LED's impart
their gnostic mystery: they tell me words
and hearing are the last to go. You've heard.

II

Under morphine he relaxed, his mouth
ajar, his breath the ruck of tearing silk:
a catch left rattling open in his throat.

His eyes half-closed, his hands clasped, twitching,
above the sheet turned down, he didn't ask
the time, he didn't ask what day it was.

A nurse came in and laved his hands and feet
in lotion, left them shiny-slick, then left.
I knew she'd done that more for me than him.

Alone, I dipped a sponge-tipped straw in water
and bathed his tongue and gums. When I withdrew
the straw he puckered after it: he knew

that much—to suck, an infant's wisdom drew
that single sign of consciousness from him.
I pled for more, but that was all he'd do.

And I was tired, and it was getting late,
I whispered that I loved him, kissed his head
and left. Ten minutes later he was dead.

[. . .]

III

Begin by saying he was gentle—how
he reached into a bird's nest on the beam
beneath the rafters of the dock, pulled back
his hand and chuckled, *There are young inside,*
inviting me to feel, but I would not—
begin with that, and note his modesty
was mild enough rebuke to vanity:
he was a man surprised he should be loved
so widely and so well, and grant him slow
to anger, too—his harshest words a curt
Be patient, to me as I held the cup
he drank from, worried it might slip and fall,
that last night in the hospital, his grip
stroke-weak. Say those were his last words to me.

Lost and Found

I

Bright sunlight on the beach across the road,
and here the stuccoed church, and here its yard,
and graves between the doorway and the curb.

We'd flown to get there, wandered down this street
the aimless way beached tourists first set out
to map anticipated ease, and found the church,

and found his single tomb: lime white, waist high
and table-flat, the slab inscribed in script—
Victorian, at length, and elegant.

We read the passage counting down the years,
months, days. He is—was—all of fifteen when
they lost him to the sea: just my age then,

you said. (But to what point? Who doesn't browse
among the stones in churchyards, thinking of
themselves?) And I was thinking back to him,

and how his body washed up on the shore,
and maybe was discovered there by those
he'd played with on the beaches as a child,

the ones who, staying close to land, survived
their intimacies with a fretful sea,
and maybe brought him home—a gift returned,

a shipwreck sacrifice, a trade for those
whose nets had filtered schools of fishes bright
as scattered coins from Caribbean blue—

a fair exchange: *We'll give you one of ours
for what we take.* So they brought back a bartered thing
returned to them, and unreturned as well.

II

Or did they find him lolling in the sea,
among the broken flotsam of the ship
that must have barked the reef in sight of shore,

in sight of help as well? Did they put out
in dinghies, once the storm had passed, to stir
among the floating salvage? Finding him

face-down and staring past the darkening depths,
what did they do—first turn him in the swell,
and watch the features coalesce beneath

the water's scrim and, maybe, given time,
take up an arm and lift and lay him out,
slack weight, and so arrange him in the hull,

a sail or net beneath, or cradle him—
the lost son, sea's child, grown a stranger—now
restored to them, their dispensation gained

and ratified, from water back to earth?
You spoke and I was one already with
the dead boy, lying underneath the carved

account of our existence, of our death:
we looked up, resting there inert, and read
the slab that said more of the grief we'd caused

than who or what we were, or how we'd come,
a remnant of a shipwreck, to this grave.
Who doesn't dream of speaking with the dead?

III

Years later, I would speak your eulogy,
the way it always goes: the young sum up,
forever clumsily, those gone ahead.

But here we read not quite the opposite—
this paragraph of names and numbers, dates
and imprecations spoke, if anything,

about the present lost than something else—
how once the grief-struck old, confronted with
their past, buried their future, young.

So we are always drowning in the dark,
and we are always washing up on shore
or being pulled, inanimate, out of the waves

and settled in the boat among the lines
and canvas, nets and floats. And we are always,
always setting out at night to scan

the smoothing surface of the water, find
what's lost, what's given up. Who doesn't look
for recompense among what's left behind?

IV

We make accommodation with the sea.
We measure it against ourselves—our tides
are not less deep or regular, our storms

more dangerous, on balance, if less broad,
our shores the interstitial arcs that bound
the waves that swell between us, lost and found.

The Second Wife

Slurs her words   and coins and candies drop
from the folds of her clothes   She interrupts the talk
to swoon at the muzak—   "Oh, Joe—remember, Joe,
The Phantom of the Opera?"   Then she leaves
to smoke in the bar,   chatting up the guy
who pours her two more drinks,   the only friend
she'll make that night.   She leans in for a kiss,
her mouth a hot pink mollusk,   wet with gin
and ostentation—how,   we wondered, did she get in?

We wondered, how did she   contrive to live
out his last days, and how   does she survive
now, diapered and confused,   the house locked up
and still while she's away,   recuperating
(that's a euphemism, though).   The shiny things
that glittered in her eyes   are gathering dust,
as her bitter sister lists   the problems to be solved.

The Sister-in-Law Sells Off the China
A Ballade

The china cabinet contains
a jumble of the old and new:
the crystal goblets, soup tureen
and serving platters share the view
with cheaper fare—a portmanteau
assortment. But what now remains
of what, the second family through,
the china cabinet contained?

The china cabinet contained
accountings of the precious things
that drew their worth from what pertained
to who we were: the napkin rings
and silver service beckoning
up memories by now constrained
to how much cash each piece will bring—
the china cabinet: contained.

Princess, understand the pains
you traffic in, and what you trade:
consider how much you've made
from what the china cabinet contained.

The Theft of the Pears

We notice first the windfalls gone:
no bees above the yellowing bellies
in the grass, no hovering buzz
above the dark late summer lawn.

So the pears go—first from the ground
below (and only one or two
left, rotten, lingering, to show
for last night's storm that cast around
the lawn the fruit and branches, leaves
now curling in the heat). Then, soon,
the lower branches have been culled,
plucked bare to arm's-reach height. We see
the untouched fruit a crown above,
a brighter, harder green among
the tangle of the branches. Neighbors
swear that they've seen no one come
or go, but then we find the tool:
a metal hoop for reaping, with
a basket underneath to catch
the fruit—and so at last we knew.

If Augustine was right, the theft
of pears is not a crime of greed,
of hunger or necessity;
our thief considered hard, prepared
ahead in easy steps, progressed
from lawn to lower branches, then
employed his reaper, reaching up
to pick at last the ripest fruit.
He stole for love of theft, because,
methodically, he loved the act.

[. . .]

In hard gold late October light,
we put the long, ash-handled tool
away: another windfall—ours.

Like Augustine, our thief may yet
repent, and meditate upon
his guilt—till then, we contemplate
uninterrupted green among
the leaves, the lawn, the absence of
the bees who've gone away to seek
out other fallen fruit now that
the theft's laid bare the thief's design,
his trespass, culling implement,
pillage—and pears no longer there.

Walking through the Empty House

In odd ungainly middle age
I rush from room to hall to room,
across the foyer, through the den,
believing, if I hurry, soon—
arriving at the place where you were then—
I'll find you there. Content to stage

imaginary drama for
a vacant house, mistaking speed
for wizardry, I hold my breath
and picture, in unreasoned need,
the chair you occupied, your death
irrelevant. Behind each door

I seek you out, believing, still,
I'll see you if I hurry and,
feet pounding on linoleum,
I barrel in, a child again,
with you expecting me to come
a-drumming through the house. I will

not find you there. These are the spells
grief bids us cast, the crazy-made
and crazy-making bargains we
transact, contrive to turn back age
and, through the doorframe, hoping, seek
what still was there when all was well.

I name each place I travel through,
replace the furniture now gone
and watch again what happened there,
stare through bare windows toward a lawn

respiring in the summer air
in memory—it's winter though,

your house is dark and empty now
and, silent, holds its breath. The heat
clicks on, the radiators sigh
and hush the drumming of my feet.
I stop. I've failed. You've not arrived.
I'm standing in an empty house.

Acknowledgments

The Very Rich Hours recounts experiences, in childhood and later, in and around my grandparents' house on Grosse Ile, Michigan, an island in the Detroit River near the mouth of Lake Erie. I am very fortunate to be able to make the following acknowledgments:

"Learning to Shave" and "Dreaming the Animal Parade" were first published in the Autumn 2008 edition of *Oberon*

"The Magnolia and the Telephone: Spring View Through the Den Window" was first published by *The Ledge* in 2009.

"Rondeaux de Chambre: Barbara's Room" was awarded Most Highly Commended status in the 2010 competition for the Margaret Reid Prize for Formal Verse.

"Crossing to Fox Island" won the Robert Frost Foundation's Robert Frost Award in October of 2009. "Walking the Dog on the Milky Way" was a runner-up in the same competition.

"The Fortune-Tellers" won an Honorable Mention in the 2010 Rita Dove Award in the Salem College International Poetry Competition.

"The Mystery of the Linen Closet "appeared in the Spring 2011 issue of *Inkwell*.

"A Paint-Crate of Photographs" appeared in the Spring 2011 issue of *The Ledge*.

"Shelling in the Philippines, World War Two" was the winner of the Poetry Prize of *The Pinch Journal* of The University of Memphis in 2009.

"Microscopy" was published, in an earlier form, in *The Sow's Ear Review* in the spring of 2010.

"The Furnace Room" and "Walking through the Empty House" won awards in the 2010 Poetry Society of Michigan Awards Competition.

"Walking the Dog on the Milky Way" first appeared in print in Alehouse in 2010. It had previously appeared online, in *The Ambassador Poetry Project*, in 2009.

"The Boat-Hoist De Profundis" was published in *The Spoon River Review* in the winter of 2009-10. It borrows a few phrases from George Herbert's "The Pulley."

"Our Musical Heritage: Time-Life Great Recordings of the Century", in slightly different form, was a winner in the 2009 Poetry Society of Michigan Competition.

"The Living Room at Night" was published online in *The Ambassador Poetry Project* in December of 2009, where "Oracle" also appeared in the Winter 2011 issue.

"A String, a Frame, a Tail" appeared in the 2011 edition of *Enizagam*.

"Lost and Found" and "The Sister-in-Law Sells Off the China: a Ballade" were first published by Pudding House Press, as part of my chapbook, *Our Parents Dancing*, in 2010.

"The Theft of the Pears" was a runner-up in the Robert Frost Foundation's 2010 Robert Frost Awards competition.

A group of related poems, "The Whole of Him Collected: A Cento and a Corona Sequence" was published as a chapbook by Finishing Line Press in 2011, and many of the poems here were collected in *About the House,* a chapbook published by Finishing Line Press in 2013.

I would also like to thank Denise Duhamel for her kind encouragement.

Praise for
The Very Rich Hours

With a haunting and contemplative voice, Loselle employs rhythm, word-play, and richness of language line after line. Through rhyme, narrative constructs, and repetition, he crafts poems that are admirably controlled and precise, and reminds us that what William Carlos Williams writes is true: "A poem is a… machine made out of words." Loselle's beautifully spun poems continue to reverberate long after the last light's been switched off.

—Janée J. Baugher, author of *The Body's Physics* and *Coördinates of Yes*

Gregory Loselle's poems offer memory illuminated by a remarkable astuteness and strong craft. In his hand, the quotidian becomes extraordinary, uncommon, and wonderful. The poet investigates with an unrelenting intelligence and an astonishing clarity.

—James Najarian, author of *The Goat Songs*

About the Author

Gregory Loselle published his first work, a play, at the age of eighteen, and subsequently won four Hopwood Awards and the Academy of American Poets Prize at The University of Michigan, where he earned an MFA. A recipient of the Ruby Lloyd Apsey Award for playwriting, he has won the William van Wert Award from Hidden River Arts and the Lorian Hemingway Short Fiction Competition for his stories, the Robert Frost Award and the Rita Dove Award for poetry.

His chapbooks, *Phantom Limb* and *Our Parents Dancing*, were published by Pudding House Press, and *The Whole of Him Collected* and *About the House* by Finishing Line Press. A fifth, *In Ordinary Time*, is forthcoming from The Moonstone Press. His poetry and short fiction has appeared widely, in print and online.

He teaches secondary Language Arts and Art History in the greater Detroit area, and can be found online at www.gloselle.com.

About The Poetry Box®

The Poetry Box was founded by Shawn Aveningo Sanders & Robert Sanders, who wholeheartedly believe that every day spent with the people you love, doing what you love, is a moment in life worth cherishing. Their boutique press celebrates the talents of their fellow artisans and writers through professional book design and publishing of individual collections, as well as their flagship literary journal, *The Poeming Pigeon*.

Feel free to visit the online bookstore (thePoetryBox.com), where you'll find more titles including:

November Quilt by Penelope Scambly Schott

Shrinking Bones by Judy K. Mosher

Epicurean Ecstasy by Cynthia Gallaher

The Poet's Curse by Michael Estabrook

Like the O in Hope by Jeanne Julian

The Unknowable Mystery of Other People by Sally Zakariya

Impossible Ledges by Dianne Avey

Painting the Heart Open by Liz Nakazawa

Bee Dance by Cathy Cain

Abruptio by Melissa Fournier

and more . . .

Printed by BoD in Norderstedt, Germany